A Maker's Guide to WEDGES

Written by JOHN WOOD

Illustrated by AMY LI

LERNER PUBLICATIONS ◆ MINNEAPOLIS

First American edition published in 2021 by Lerner Publishing Group, Inc.

© 2021 Booklife Publishing

Editor: Madeline Tyler
Design: Amy Li

Lerner Publications Company
An imprint of Lerner Publishing Group, Inc.
241 First Avenue North
Minneapolis, MN 55401 USA

For reading levels and more information, look up this title at www.lernerbooks.com.

Main body text set in VAG Rounded Std. Typeface provided by Adobe Systems.

Library of Congress Cataloging-in-Publication Data

Names: Wood, John, 1990- author. | Li, Amy, illustrator.
Title: A maker's guide to wedges / written by John Wood ; illustrated by Amy Li.
Other titles: Wedges
Description: First American edition. | Minneapolis : Lerner Publications, 2021. | Series: A maker's guide to simple machines | Includes index. | Audience: Ages 6–10 | Audience: Grades 2–3 | Summary: "Join the Maker, an alien who knows all about machines, and take a look at wedges. Readers will learn about different types of wedges and how they help make life on Earth easier"— Provided by publisher.
Identifiers: LCCN 2020054219 (print) | LCCN 2020054220 (ebook) | ISBN 9781728416458 (lib. bdg.) | ISBN 9781728438344 (pbk.) | ISBN 9781728418902 (eb pdf)
Subjects: LCSH: Wedges—Juvenile literature.
Classification: LCC TJ1201.W44 W658 2021 (print) | LCC TJ1201.W44 (ebook) | DDC 621.8—dc23

LC record available at https://lccn.loc.gov/2020054219
LC ebook record available at https://lccn.loc.gov/2020054220

Manufactured in the United States of America
1-48892-49206-12/28/2020

Table of CONTENTS

Words that look like this can be found in the glossary on page 24.

BE A MAKER

Oh dear! What a mess—Maker is a very clumsy alien. Say sorry, Maker.

PFFLBLUBWUBLEE.

Believe it or not, Maker is very smart when it comes to machines.

A machine is an object that makes a job easier to do. Maker wants to teach you about one of the simplest types of machine: a wedge.

A stapler is a simple machine. So is a door.

5

WEDGES

A wedge is something that is very thick at one end and very thin at the other. Wedges can hold things together or split things apart.

Wedges are often shaped like a triangle.

Wedges are often used to split something apart. For example, an axe is a wedge. Axes are often used to split wood apart.

The thin end of an axe is sharp.

HEUFFFLiPUGHHt.

Here are some more examples of wedges that people use.

KNIFE

CHISEL

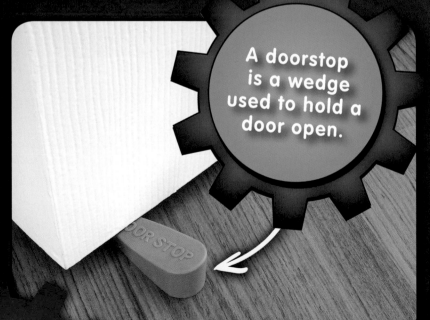

A doorstop is a wedge used to hold a door open.

DOOR STOP

A nail is a type of wedge.

Did you know that there is a type of wedge that you have, but Maker doesn't?

FLYBLIFFLENYLEUGH.

The answer is teeth!

Teeth split food apart.

PARTS OF A WEDGE

Many wedges are like two <u>ramps</u> stuck together. One end is thick and wide. The other is thin and sometimes sharp. It is the thin end that splits or holds something.

Thick end

Thin end

Something or someone must use <u>force</u> to move the wedge. For example, a person might use their strength to swing an axe into a tree.

Sometimes wedges are moved by <u>motors</u>, such as this nail gun.

HOW DOES A WEDGE WORK?

A wedge changes the <u>direction</u> of the force. When a person swings an axe down, the bits of wood are moved sideways. Can you see how the direction of the force changes in the picture?

Sometimes the wedge is forced in by hitting it with another **tool**, such as a hammer.

It is much easier to swing an axe downward than it is to pull wood apart. This is why a wedge is such a good simple machine. It makes the work much easier.

SINGLES OR DOUBLES

Wedges come in two types: single wedges and double wedges. In a double wedge, force is <u>redirected</u> in two directions. Most of the wedges we have looked at so far have been double wedges.

In a double wedge, both sides go from thick to thin.

Doorstops and chisels are examples of single wedges. In a single wedge, one side goes from thick to thin, but the other side is flat. This means the force is only changed in one direction.

Thick

Thin

Flat side

HEUEBLUPHREE!

THE BEST WEDGE

Maker, what makes a good wedge?

FYRIPPLEYRIPLI.

Ah, interesting. Maker says it has to do with the distance between the thick end and the thin end, and how sharp it is.

The longer and sharper a wedge is, the less force it will take for the work to get done. A shorter wedge will need more force.

This is a long wedge!

BUILD A TOY CROCODILE

It is time to build! We will be using wedges to make a toy crocodile with teeth. Remember, teeth are a type of wedge.

YOU WILL NEED:

- 2 pieces of green construction paper
- Glue
- A piece of cardboard
- 2 googly eyes
- Scissors
- A pen or pencil

You will need an adult to help you when using scissors and glue.

Fold one-third of one piece of paper lengthwise. Cover it in glue, and then fold the other side on top.

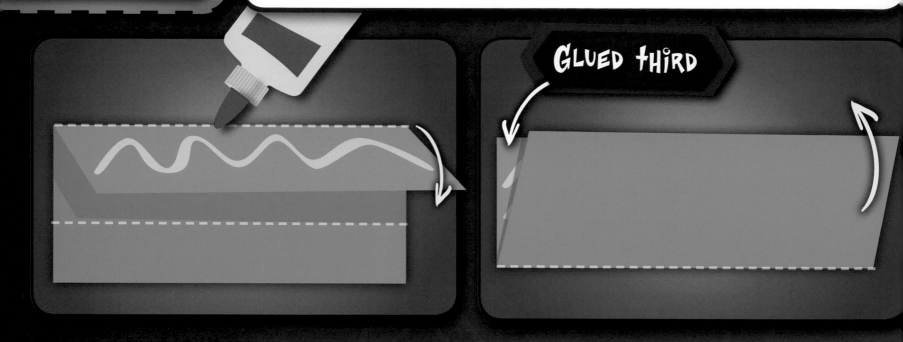

GLUED THIRD

Fold the paper so it is half as long. Fold the open ends down so that they touch the fold line.

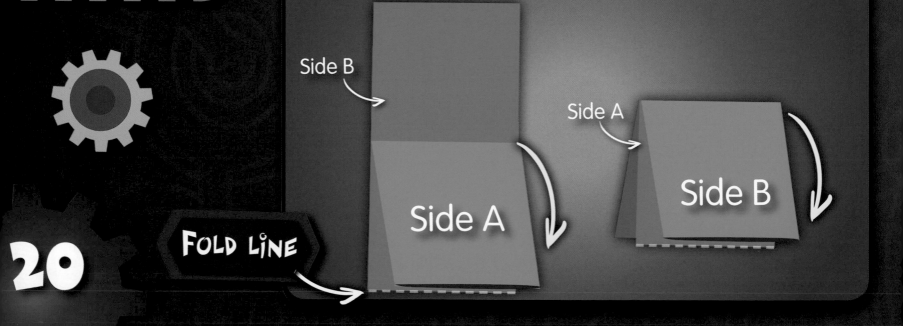

Side B

Side A

Side A

Side B

FOLD LINE

Cut the other paper into thirds lengthwise. Take one strip and fold it back and forth until it looks like the picture.

STEP 4

Glue the two pieces together, like in the picture. The open ends of the first piece should face the long strip.

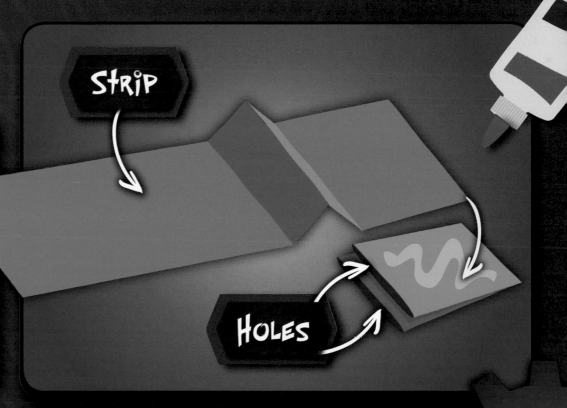

STRIP

HOLES

Glue two eyes onto the part that sticks up. Fold the long strip back and forth to make a zigzag, and then cut it into a point to make the tail.

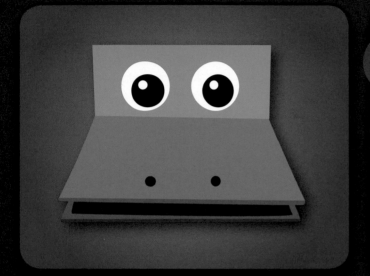

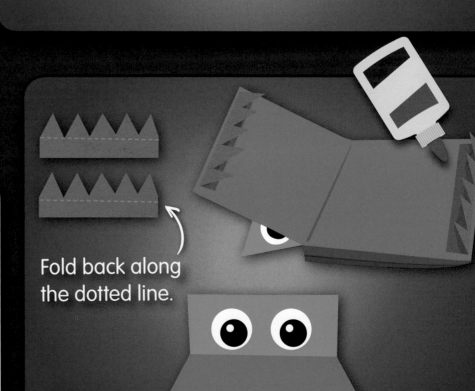

STEP 6

Cut two rows of spikes out of your cardboard. These are your teeth. Glue them to the front of the mouth, like the picture.

Fold back along the dotted line.

STEP 7

Put your fingers and thumb into the holes under the tail. Now you can make the crocodile bite.

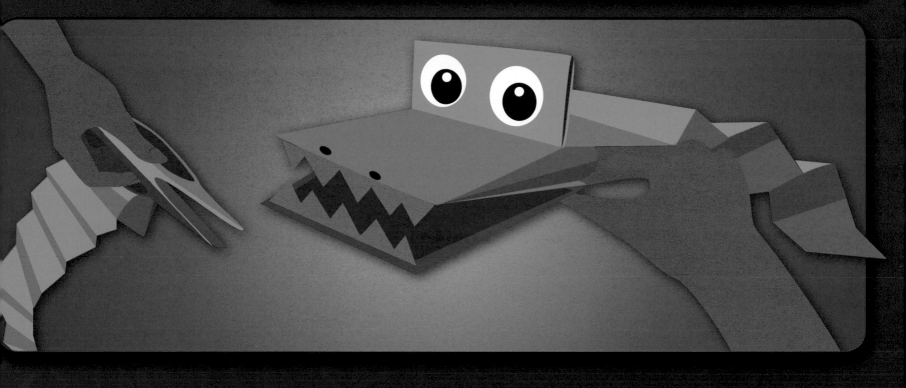

STEP 8

Test out your crocodile on different materials. Can you bite into something soft?

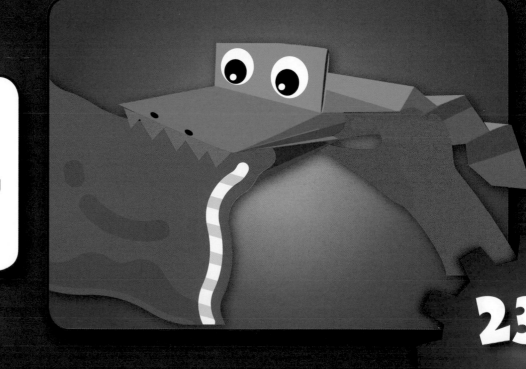

23

GLOSSARY

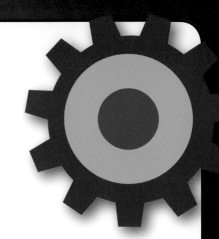

direction   a course along which something is moving

force   a push or pull on an object

motors   machines that move things

ramps   sloping planes connecting different levels

redirected   changed direction

tool   an object used to do a certain job

INDEX